THIS BOOK
BELONGS TO

_____

_____

_____

THE SIMPSONS 2015 ANNUAL

Copyright © 2014
Bongo Entertainment, Inc. All rights reserved.
No part of this book may be used or reproduced in any manner whatsoever
without written permission except in the case of brief quotations
embodied in critical articles and reviews. For information address
Bongo Comics Group
P.O. Box 1963, Santa Monica, CA 90406-1963

Published in the UK by Titan Books, a division of Titan Publishing Group,
144 Southwark St., London SE1 0UP, under licence from Bongo Entertainment, Inc.

FIRST EDITION: SEPTEMBER 2014

ISBN 9781783291571

2 4 6 8 10 9 7 5 3 1

Publisher: Matt Groening
Creative Director: Nathan Kane
Managing Editor: Terry Delegeane
Director of Operations: Robert Zaugh
Art Director: Chia-Hsien Jason Ho
Art Director Special Projects: Serban Cristescu
Production Manager: Christopher Ungar
Assistant Art Director: Mike Rote
Assistant Editor: Karen Bates
Colors: Nathan Hamill, Art Villanueva
Administration: Ruth Waytz, Pete Benson
Legal Guardian: Susan A. Grode

PRINTED IN ITALY

THE SIMPSONS™ ANNUAL 2015

TITAN BOOKS

EVERYBODY LOVES A PARADE

UP AND AT 'EM, MARGE! TODAY'S THE SPRINGFIELD CHRISTMAS...I MEAN, *HOLIDAY*...I MEAN, *WINTER*...I MEAN *COLD TIME* PARADE!

LARD LAD HAS A *DONUT CANNON* THIS YEAR TO SHOOT *FREE DONUTS* INTO THE CROWD! WE NEED TO GET THERE *EARLY* AND GRAB A GOOD SPOT!

OH, HOMIE... IT'S *TWO A.M.!*

MATT GROENING

♪ SILVER BELLS, ♪ SILVER BELLS, IT'S *WAKE UP* TIME IN ♪ THE CITY! ♪

♪ DING DONG! DING DONG! ♪

WHAT IN THE NAME OF ST. NICHOLAS ARE YOU DOING, HOMER?!?

LET'S SEE WHAT'S IN THE PAPER TODAY... *WHAAAT?!* SANTA'S REINDEER ALLEGE *ANIMAL ABUSE?!*

⸘GASP!⸘ CALL THE *SPCA!* CALL *PETA!* CALL... CALL...

J. TORRES
WRITER

JOHN DELANEY
PENCILS

ANDREW PEPOY
INKS

NATHAN HAMILL
COLORS

KAREN BATES
LETTERS

NATHAN KANE
EDITOR

8

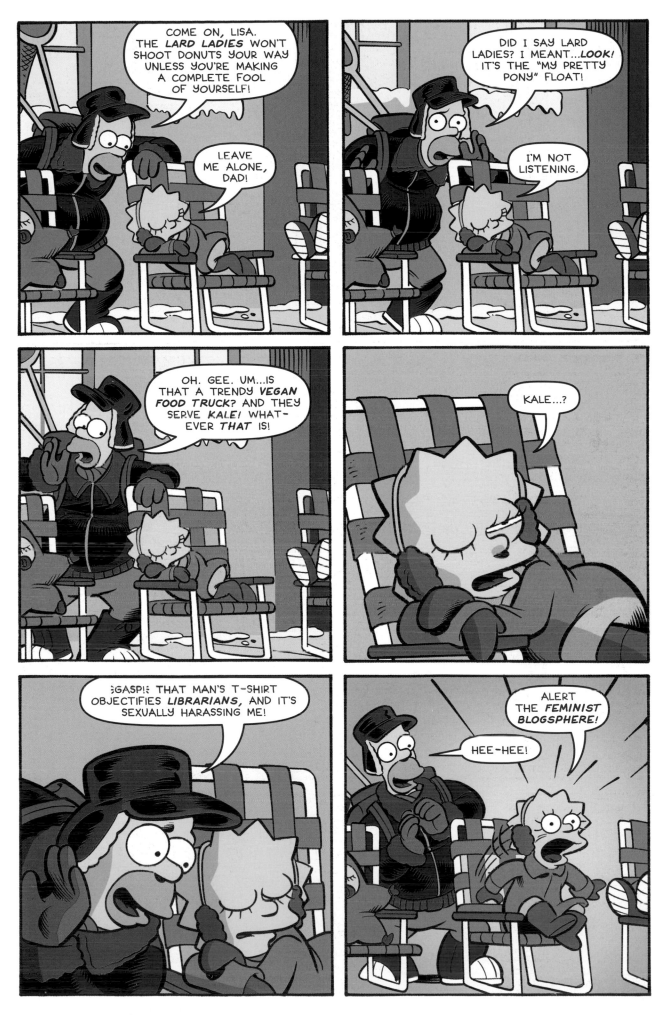

9

15

PETE ZA PARTY

SHANE HOUGHTON
WRITER

HILARY BARTA
ART

ART VILLANUEVA
COLORS

KAREN BATES
LETTERS

NATHAN KANE
EDITOR

THE NEXT DAY...

HEY, WHAT ARE YOU GUYS DOING IN HERE?

BURNS IS MAKIN' *CUTBACKS*.

WE'RE ALL *SHARING* A WORKSTATION NOW.

SO OLD MAN BURNS IS PLAYING HARDBALL, EH? HEH...A *MINOR BLOW* TO MY NAP SCHEDULE. I'VE FALLEN ASLEEP UNDER WORSE CONDITIONS.

DON'T DRINK THAT! INSTEAD OF COFFEE GROUNDS, BURNS IS JUST USING THE *DIRT* THAT COFFEE BEANS GROW IN.

HAS A GRITTY, MOCHA TASTE THOUGH.

EH. I'M OFF FOR MY MID-MORNING "READING" BREAK. I'LL SEE YOU GUYS IN FORTY MINUTES.

SWAT!

22

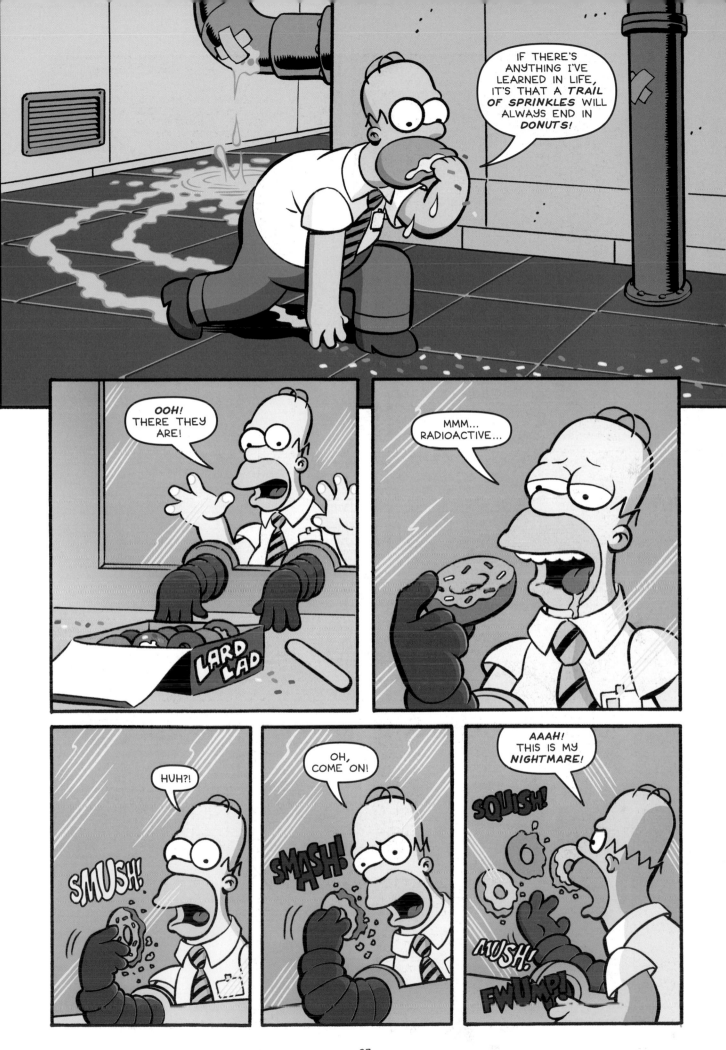

23

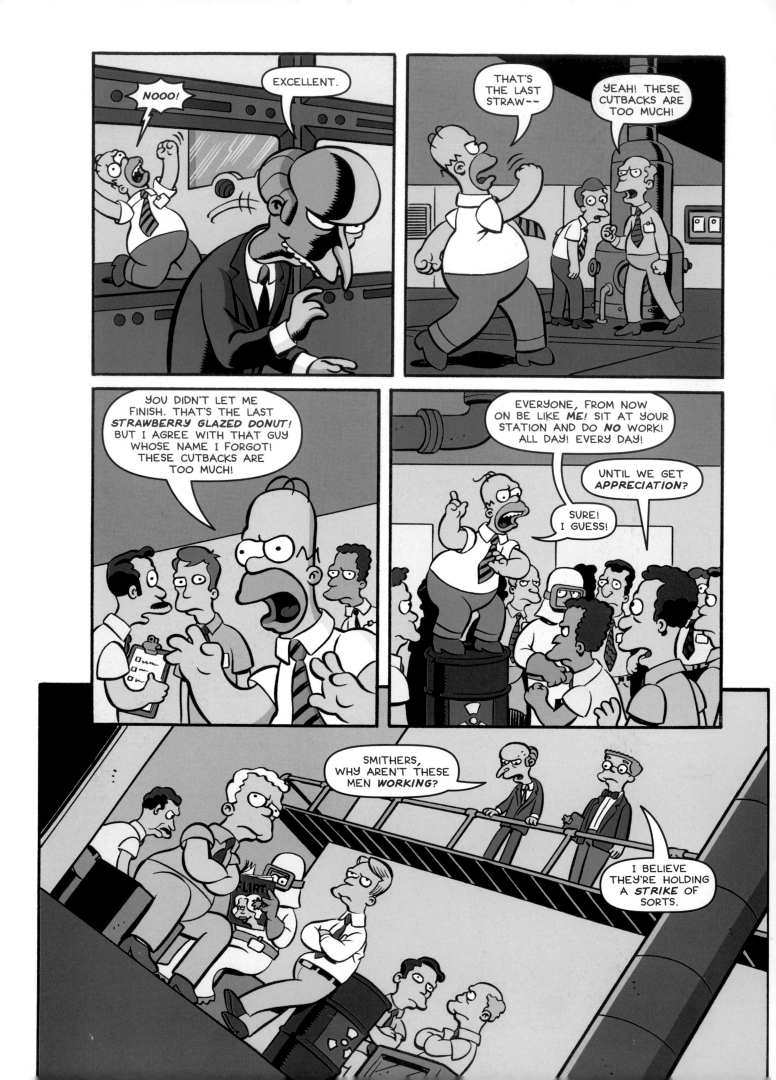

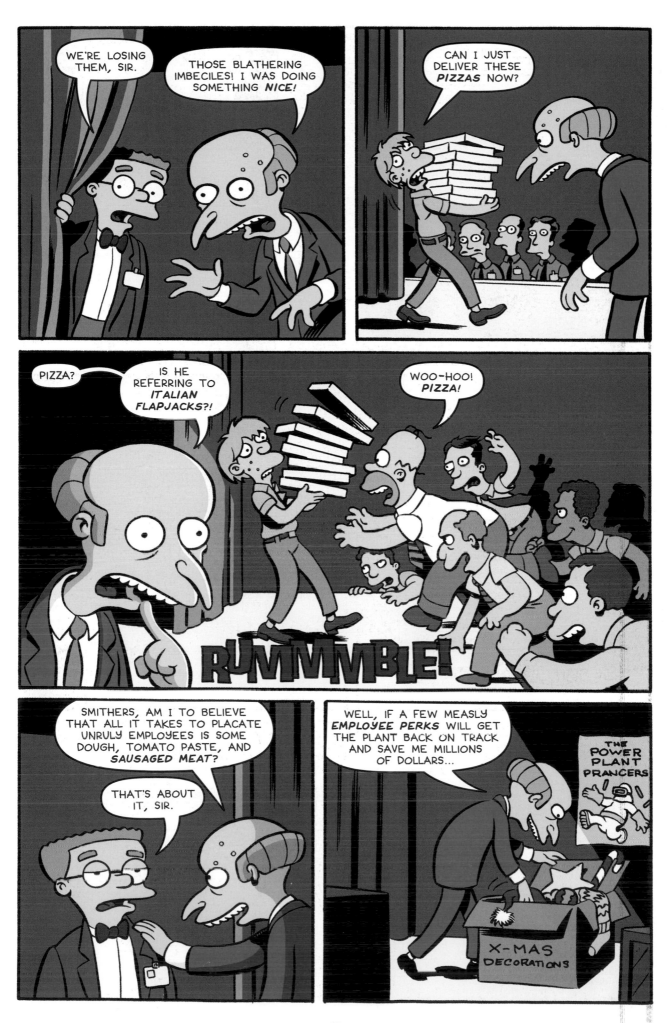

28

JAMES W. BATES
SCRIPT

JOEY NILGES
PENCILS

MIKE ROTE
INKS

NATHAN HAMILL
COLORS

KAREN BATES
LETTERS

BILL MORRISON
EDITOR

I CAN SMELL THE STEWED PRUNES FROM HERE.

SCREEEECH!

OKAY, BART. TRY TO STAY POSITIVE. MAYBE THIS WON'T BE SO BAD.

WHO ARE YOU KIDDING?

HUH?

POSITIVE THINKING WON'T HELP YOU. THIS PLACE IS A YAWNER. ALL THESE FOSSILS DO IS SIT AROUND AND WAIT FOR THE REAPER TO COME.

YOU'RE A KID. YOU SHOULD BE OUT RUNNING AROUND OR AT HOME PLAYING VIDEO GAMES AND EATING CANDY.

TRUST ME, I KNOW!

WANT SOME? I CONFISCATED IT FROM ONE OF THE OLD GUYS. I TRICKED HIM BY TELLING HIM HE WAS ON A RESTRICTED DIET! HA!

UH...NO, THANKS.

YOUR LOSS! THEY'RE PRETTY GOOB ...I MEAN GOOD...BUT THEY DO GET STUCK IN YOUR TEETH.

I'M HERE TO VISIT WITH MY GRAMPA...ABE SIMPSON.

33

MAX DAVISON
WRITER

JAMES LLOYD
PENCILS

STEVE STEERE, JR.
INKS

ART VILLANUEVA
COLORS

KAREN BATES
LETTERS

NATHAN KANE
EDITOR

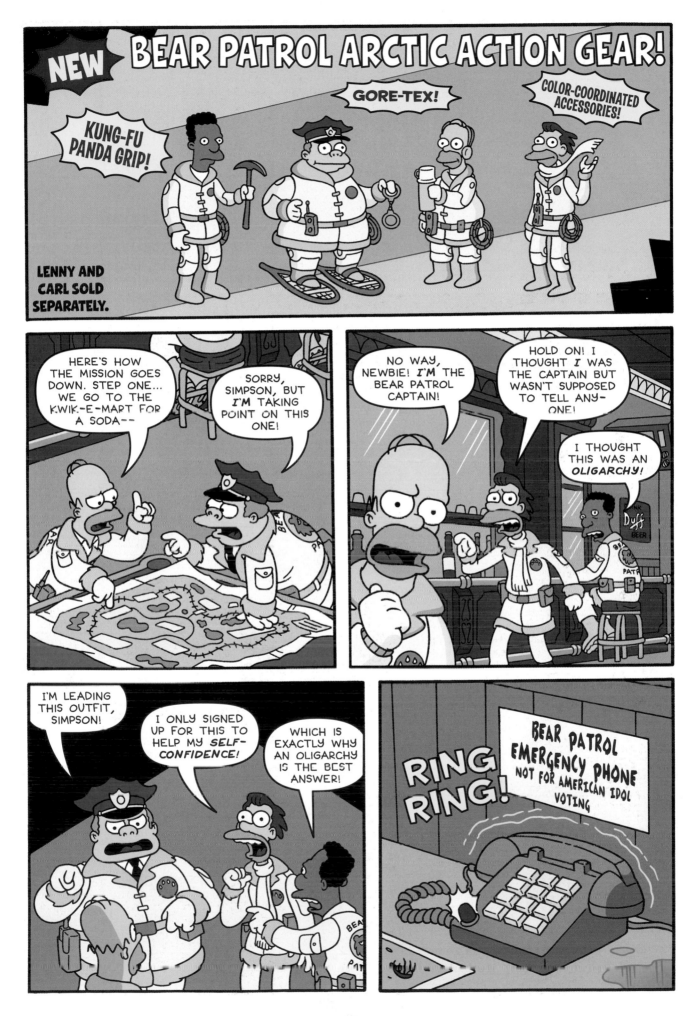

DON'T MIND US. JUST PART OF THE ECOSYSTEM!

STILL NOT SURE WHY I COULDN'T JUST WEAR THE OTHER SNOWMAN SUIT.

HEH HEH!

COAL BIN

TIME FOR *PLAN A!* RECKLESSLY CHARGING INTO THE HOUSE!

THE ONLY WAY IN SEEMS TO BE THAT CHIMNEY!

FOLLOW MY LEAD!

NOT IF I GET THERE FIRST!

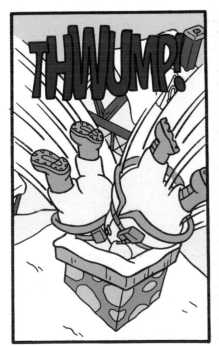

THWUMP!

HMM. THIS *COULD* TAKE SOME TIME.

ONE THOROUGHLY UNCOMFORTABLE SLIDE LATER...

OKAY. TIME TO UNLEASH MY *SECRET WEAPON!*

47

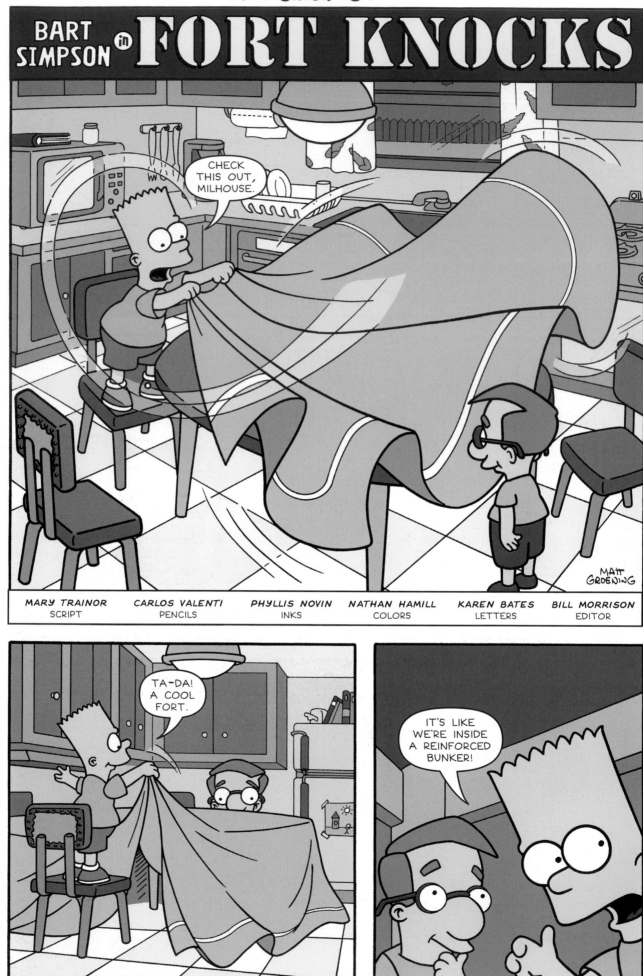

53

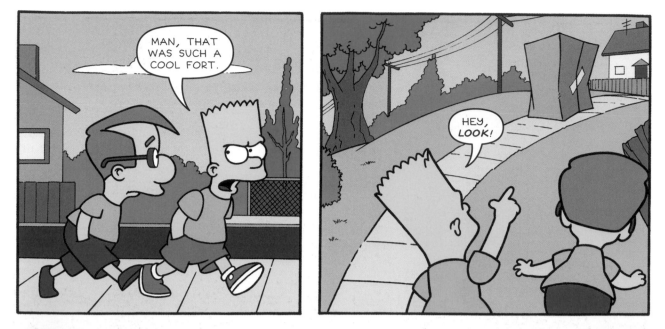

QUICK! IN HERE!

HEY, MILHOUSE, YOU KNOW WHAT? THIS MAKES A COOL FORT!

THE END

D.I.Y. HOMER

MATT GROENING

SHANE HOUGHTON
WRITER

REX LINDSEY
PENCILS

DAN DAVIS
INKS

ART VILLANUEVA
COLORS

KAREN BATES
LETTERS

NATHAN KANE
EDITOR

64